DK

MARES MEMORIAL LIBRARY/DICKINSON

3 4050 00080 0107

D0623674

11/06

Mares Memorial Library
4324 Highway 3
Dickinson, TX 77539

DEMCO

MUSICAL INSTRUMENTS OF THE WORLD

Keyboards

M. J. Knight

Mares Memorial Library
4324 Highway 3
Dickinson, TX 77539

Smart Apple Media

Published by Smart Apple Media
2140 Howard Drive West, North Mankato, Minnesota 56003

Designed by Helen James

Photographs by Edwin Beunk, Corbis (Nubar Alexanian, Bettmann, Burstein Collection, Christie's Images, DELLA ZUANA PASCAL/CORBIS SYGMA, Henry Diltz, DUGOWSON/STM CONCEPT/CORBIS SYGMA, RUSSEIL CHRISTOPHE/CORBIS SYGMA, Marc Garanger, Francoise Gervais, Philip Gould, Hulton-Deutsch Collection, Bob Krist, Charles & Jesette Lenars, Roy McMahon, Francis G. Mayer, Gianni Dagli Orti, Jose F. Poblete), The Lebrecht Collection

Copyright © 2006 Smart Apple Media. International copyrights reserved in all countries. No part of this book may be reproduced in any form without written permission from the publisher.

Printed in Thailand

Library of Congress Cataloging-in-Publication Data

Knight, M. J.
Keyboards / by M. J. Knight.
p. cm. — (Musical instruments of the world)
Includes index.
ISBN 1-58340-412-0
1. Keyboard instruments—Juvenile literature. [1. Keyboard instruments.] I. Title. II. Musical instruments (North Mankato, Minn.)

ML549.K6 2004
786'.19—dc22   2003067398

First Edition

9 8 7 6 5 4 3 2 1

3 4050 00080 0107

Contents

Introducing Keyboards

Keyboards Keyboards

This book is about instruments with keyboards. Keyboard instruments all sound when their keys are pressed. The sounds are made in various ways.

Some of the oldest keyboard instruments, such as the harpsichord, sound when quills pluck the strings inside. The piano also has strings inside, but they are struck by small, felt-covered hammers to sound the notes.

A church organ has pipes that sound notes when air is pushed through them. An electronic organ creates notes from electric signals when its keys are pressed.

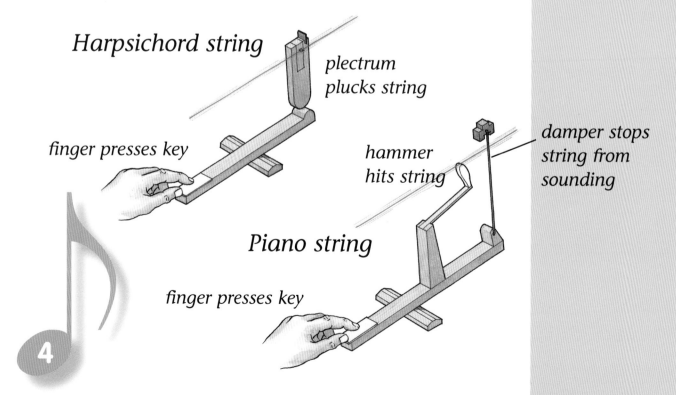

Harpsichord string

plectrum plucks string

finger presses key

hammer hits string

damper stops string from sounding

Piano string

finger presses key

You can hear keyboard instruments play all sorts of music in all sorts of places. Pianists perform classical music in concerts and also accompany singers and other solo instruments. Jazz and dance music often have parts for a piano, too.

The accordion and hurdy gurdy are traditional folk instruments. Their sound is loud, so they are often played outside at festivals and fairs.

Electronic organs and keyboards of many different kinds play a part in many pop and rock bands today. You can hear them on the radio, on CD, or live in concert.

A singer is accompanied by a pianist playing a grand piano.

5

Clavichord

Clavichord Clavichord Clavichord Clavichord

The oldest of all the keyboard instruments is the clavichord. It looks like an oblong wooden box with a lid that opens. Inside the box, pairs of metal strings are stretched lengthwise, from end to end.

The keyboard of a clavichord is set toward the left-hand side. When you press a key, a small metal blade called a tangent hits a pair of strings and sounds a note.

The clavichord has a very quiet voice, and its sound is soft and gentle. Five hundred years ago, it was the first keyboard instrument that people learned to play at home.

Arnold Dolmetsch, who made clavichords and harpsichords in the early 1900s, carrying a clavichord with his wife.

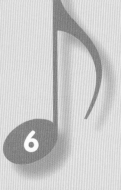

Virginal Virginal Virginal Virginal

Like the clavichord, the virginal is an old instrument that was first played nearly 500 years ago. It is shaped like a box and is often played on a table.

The keyboard of the virginal is small, and it can be located at either end of the casing or in the middle. When you press a key, a small quill (the hard middle part of a feather) plucks a string to sound a gentle, tinkling note.

Many virginals are beautifully decorated, with paintings of flowers or country landscapes on the lid and wooden casing.

This 200-year-old painting shows a woman sitting in front of a decorated virginal.

Harpsichord Harpsichord

Have you ever heard a harpsichord? It has a clear, crisp tone and can make a powerful sound. This beautiful old instrument looks a bit like a slender grand piano. Its triangular-shaped outer casing stands on four slim legs.

Harpsichords may have more than one keyboard. When you press a key, a small quill called a plectrum plucks the strings inside to make a note. There are two or more strings for each key.

This old French painting shows a woman accompanying two string players on the harpsichord.

8

Did You Know?

The quills inside a harpsichord were made from the wing and tail feathers of various birds, including crows, ravens, turkeys, and eagles. Today, they are usually made of plastic.

A harpsichord maker fits a key into place in a harpsichord with two keyboards.

A harpsichord player can choose the number of strings to play by pulling out a small lever called a stop. If the player uses all the strings, the music is loud. Using fewer strings makes the music softer.

Today, you hear the harpsichord only occasionally, but 500 years ago, many people played it. It also played an important part in orchestras during the 1700s.

Spinet Spinet Spinet Spinet

Little sister to the harpsichord is the spinet. Three hundred years ago, people played the spinet at home, partly because it was small and fit easily into their homes.

Most spinets are triangular-shaped, with the keyboard on the shortest side of the triangle. When you press a key, a tiny quill plucks a string inside to sound the note. The sound is quiet and tinkling.

To make the sound louder, the wooden lid is propped up while the spinet is played.

A woman plays the spinet as two men listen in this painting.

10

This is the name of an early version of the piano we know today. It was invented about 300 years ago by an Italian named Bartolomeo Cristofori, who also built harpsichords.

Cristofori's new instrument looked like the harpsichord. The main difference was in the way the sound was made. When you pressed the keys of the fortepiano, the strings were hit by small hammers instead of being plucked by quills. This made a very different sound and meant that the fortepiano could be played much louder than the harpsichord.

Can you see the difference between the keys on this fortepiano and the ones on the piano on page 14?

Fortepiano

Grand piano Grand piano

Gran

True to its name, this piano is very grand! The largest grand pianos are nearly 10 feet (3 m) long. They are called concert grands. Smaller grand pianos are called baby grands.

Grand pianos are made of wood and have a strong iron frame inside to hold the strings. During a concert, the lid over the strings is propped open to make the sound louder.

When a pianist presses a key, a small hammer strikes a string inside to sound a note.

This pianist is playing a grand piano with the lid propped open.

When a pianist presses a key, a felt-tipped hammer hits a string inside to make a sound.

Piano strings are of different thicknesses: thick strings on the left side play low notes, and thinner ones on the right side play higher notes. When the pianist lifts his or her finger off a key, a small pad called a damper falls against the string to stop its sound.

Did You Know?

The winged shape of a grand piano is designed around the strings. The long bass (low) strings are on the left, and the shorter treble (high) strings are on the right.

The grand piano has pedals that the pianist presses with his or her feet to change the sound of the notes. The right pedal keeps all the dampers away from the strings and is called the sustaining pedal. Pressing it makes the sound of the piano fuller and richer. The left pedal makes the notes softer and quieter.

Upright piano
Upright piano

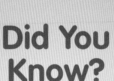

Are you learning to play the piano? If so, you are probably learning on an upright piano. This piano is named for its shape. It sits against a wall and takes up much less space than its bigger cousin, the grand piano.

When you press a key on the piano, a small hammer hits a string inside to sound a note. The piano has two pedals that you press with your feet: one makes the note longer and richer, while the other makes it softer.

Did You Know?

Inside the piano, the strings are stretched very tightly over a strong iron frame. Behind it is a soundboard that makes the vibrations of the strings louder.

This boy is practicing on an upright piano.

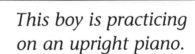

The melodica is a type of mouth organ and sounds much like an organ. You play it through a mouthpiece at one end.

The piano melodica has a set of keys along its length. As you blow into the mouthpiece, you push these keys down to play a tune with the fingers of one hand.

Inside the melodica are thin pieces of metal called reeds. When the air you blow into the mouthpiece moves across the reeds, they vibrate to make notes.

You can see the unusual mouthpiece being played on this melodica.

Accordion Accordion Accordion

The accordion is a complicated instrument to play. You have to be strong to squeeze the pleated folds in the middle (called bellows) in and out. The squeezing pushes air over a set of reeds, which make the notes.

While squeezing the bellows, the accordionist plays a tune with his right hand. Each key plays two different notes—one when the bellows are squeezed together, and a different one when they are pulled apart.

An accordion player squeezes the bellows and plays the keyboard at the same time.

The accordionist uses his left hand to press the finger buttons on the other side of the bellows. These sound chords as an accompaniment to the tune.

The accordion was invented nearly 200 years ago in Germany. Today, you can hear it playing folk music in Europe and North and South America. It is an important instrument in cajun and zydeco music, which both grew out of the traditional folk music of Louisiana.

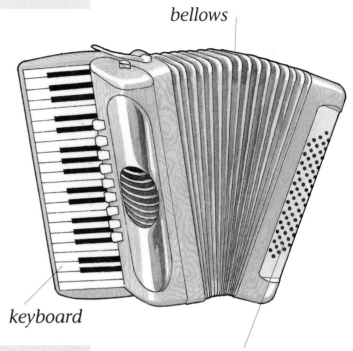

bellows

keyboard

finger buttons

Accordion Accordion Accordion

Did You Know?

An old name for the accordion is the squeeze-box, because you have to squeeze it to play it.

Dulcitone

Dulcitone Dulcitone
Dulcitone Dulcitone

The sound of the dulcitone is soft and bell-like. This small wooden instrument stands on four slim legs.

Inside the dulcitone is a row of U-shaped metal bars of different sizes. When you press a key, a small hammer hits one of the bars to sound a note.

A dulcitone is simple in appearance but has a beautiful sound.

The dulcitone was invented in the 1800s by a Frenchman named Auguste Mustel, who lived in Paris. Its original name was the tuning fork piano.

Celeste Celeste Celeste

The celeste looks a bit like an upright piano, but it makes a very different, bell-like sound when played.

Inside the wooden case are a row of steel bars. When you press a key, a tiny, felt-covered hammer hits one of the bars. Underneath each bar is a small, hollow box that makes the sound louder. A foot pedal called the sustaining pedal makes the notes longer when you press it.

You can hear the celeste in the ballet *The Nutcracker*, written by the Russian composer Tchaikovsky. Listen for it in "The Dance of the Sugar Plum Fairy."

The celeste has just one foot pedal, which is used to make the sound louder.

Organ Organ Organ

The organ is one of the oldest and loudest musical instruments in the world. It has a row of pipes that sound notes when air is pushed through them. The smallest organ pipes are just a few inches long, while the longest are more than 64 feet (19 m) long.

There are two types of organ pipes, and they make different sounds. Flue pipes are open pipes with a mouthpiece. They can be open at one end or closed (stopped). A stopped pipe makes a

This beautiful organ in Germany has 17,000 pipes and is one of the largest organs in the world.

lower note than an open pipe. The other pipes are called reed pipes and have thin metal reeds inside that sound when air passes over them.

Organs have one or more keyboards called manuals. Each keyboard is linked to rows of pipes that have levers called stops. The stops have names, such as flute or trumpet, that describe the sound they make when the organist pulls them out.

The biggest organs played today are in churches and cathedrals.

An organist playing on two different keyboards, or manuals, at the same time.

Did You Know?

Many years ago, the air that makes the organ play had to be pumped into the organ by hand through a set of bellows. Today, it is pumped by an electric motor.

Harmonium

Harmonium

Harmonium

A harmonium sounds a bit like an organ. It is sometimes called the reed organ, because the sound it makes comes from a series of metal reeds.

When air is pushed over the reeds, notes are produced. The air is pumped into the instrument by a set of bellows that the harmonium player pushes with his feet.

The harmonium was invented about 200 years ago in France. It was often played in churches that did not have an organ, or in people's homes.

A Russian monk playing the harmonium in a monastery.

Ondes martenot

The ondes martenot is an electronic instrument invented in the 1920s by a Frenchman named Maurice Martenot.

The keyboard is connected to speakers. When you press a key, a note is created electronically, then amplified (made louder) through the speakers. The sound is a strange, eerie wailing, halfway between a hum and a voice singing "oo."

The ondes martenot also has controls to make the notes louder, softer, or different in other ways. You can sometimes hear it in movie soundtracks.

Did You Know?

The word *ondes* is French for "waves." The inventor used it to describe the smooth falling and rising sound of his instrument.

Maurice Martenot's sister, Ginette, playing the ondes martenot.

Hurdy gurdy

This ancient instrument looks like a thick and chunky violin with a handle at one end. When you turn the handle, it turns a wheel underneath the strings and makes them vibrate.

On the side of the hurdy gurdy is a small keyboard. Pushing down the keys moves small wooden blades that press against the strings to make different notes.

A musician playing the hurdy gurdy at a street festival in France.

24

Hurdy gurdy

Hurdy gurdy

As shown in this old painting, the hurdy gurdy has not changed much over the years.

The hurdy gurdy usually has between four and six strings. Two of them play a single long note called a drone. The other strings play the tune, or melody.

Players hang the hurdy gurdy around their neck from a strap, or sit down to play with the instrument on their lap.

The first hurdy gurdys were played in medieval times. Traveling musicians called minstrels often played the hurdy gurdy because it was easy to carry around with them. Today, you can hear it playing traditional folk music.

25

Pianola Pianola

Imagine a piano that plays itself! This is just what the pianola does. It looks like an ordinary upright piano, but it has a roll of paper set into the wooden casing above the keyboard.

The paper roll has holes punched in it. It turns automatically, and the holes act like a code that tells the piano which notes to play.

Some pianolas are worked by bellows that the pianist pushes with her feet. The bellows blow air that turns the paper roll. Other pianolas run on electricity.

This old drawing is trying to show that the pianola is easy to play— even a baby can press down the bellows.

Electronic organ

An organist accompanying gospel singers at a jazz festival.

The electronic organ has no pipes. Instead, it makes notes from signals produced by electricity. The signals are amplified and heard through speakers.

Electronic organs often have two keyboards, called manuals. They also have switches called stops, which the player can press to make an enormous range of sounds. Drums and percussion sounds are built in to accompany the tune the organist is playing.

You can hear the electronic organ played in many rock and pop bands.

Did You Know?

In June 2000, music students in Hungary set a record for the largest number of keyboards ever played at once. They played 100 electronic keyboards programmed to sound like the different instruments of an orchestra.

Keyboards in concert

Where can you hear keyboards? They play all sorts of music in places all over the world.

In classical music, the piano often accompanies singers and solo instruments. You can also hear the piano as a solo instrument—in a piece of music called a piano concerto, for example. Many famous classical composers were also brilliant pianists, such as Beethoven, Mozart, and Liszt.

Years ago, popular dance bands almost always included a piano. During the early 1900s, many people spent

A pianist and composer performing at a festival in France.

STEINWAY & SONS

Keyboards in concert

A rock musician using keyboards to make electronic music on a synthesizer.

evenings out dancing to a band. These bands often also had a clarinet, a double bass, and drums to beat out the rhythm.

Pianos play a big part in many jazz bands, too. Jazz music originated in America from traditional work songs and spirituals. In jazz, each instrument plays its own tune, and the musicians often improvise, or make up the notes as they go. Jazz music spread throughout America and the rest of the world during the 1900s. There are many different types of jazz, and today you can hear it played everywhere. Famous jazz pianists have included Scott Joplin, Jelly Roll Morton, Duke Ellington, and Fats Waller.

Today's rock bands often have an electronic piano or organ that is accompanied by electric guitars and drums.

Words to Remember

accompany To play music alongside a singer or another musician who is playing the tune.

amplified Made louder.

bands Groups of musicians playing together.

bellows Part of an instrument that holds air. You squeeze bellows to pump air through an instrument (such as an organ or accordion) to make it sound.

casing The outer part of a keyboard instrument.

chords Groups of notes played together.

classical music Serious music is sometimes called classical music to separate it from popular music. Classical music can also mean music that was written during the late 18th and early 19th centuries and follows certain rules.

composer Someone who writes pieces of music.

concerts Performances in front of an audience.

folk music Traditional songs and tunes that are so old that no one remembers who wrote them.

jazz A type of music played by a group of instruments in which each one plays its own tune. Jazz musicians often improvise, or make up, the tunes they play.

keyboard The row of keys on a keyboard instrument.

keys Parts of a keyboard that move a lever to sound a note.

musicians People who play instruments or sing.

orchestras Groups of about 90 musicians who play classical music together.

pedals Parts of an instrument worked by foot.

pop Popular music that is entertaining and easy to listen to.

quills The hard middle parts of birds' feathers, used to pluck strings on a harpsichord or virginal.

reeds Small, thin pieces of metal that vibrate to make a note.

rhythm The beat of the music, which depends on how short or long the notes are.

rock Pop music with a strong beat, or rhythm.

solo A piece of music played or sung by one performer.

spirituals Religious songs that began among black slaves in the southern United States more than 200 years ago.

stop A lever or knob that changes the sound of some instruments when pulled.

tone The sound of an instrument.

vibrate To move up and down quickly, or to quiver.

Index